Serpent in the Sanctuary
How the Devil Wages War Against the Church

Serpent in the Sanctuary
How the Devil Wages War Against the Church

by
Archbishop Paul M. French

COPYRIGHT © 2026 by Paul M French
All rights reserved. This book or any portion thereof may not be reproduced or used in any manner whatsoever without the express written permission of the author except for the use of brief quotations in a book review.

All rights reserved. No part of this publication may be reproduced, stored in or introduced into a retrieval system, or transmitted, in any form, or by any means (electrical, mechanical, photocopying, recording, or otherwise) without the prior written consent of the author. Any person who does any unauthorized act in relation to this publication may be liable to criminal prosecution civil claims for damages.

Title of Book: Serpent in the Sanctuary – How the Devil Wages War Against the Church by Paul M. French

ISBN 13: 979-8-218-94478-0

1. Religion. 2. Roman Catholicism. 3. Anglicanism. Serpent in the Sanctuary – How the Devil Wages War Against the Church

Cover Design by: IWNH, LLC

Printed in the United States of America

Preface

The story of the Church in the modern West is, in many ways, a story of paradox. On the one hand, Christ has promised that the gates of hell shall not prevail against His Church. On the other, the most visible expressions of that Church appear shaken by scandal, divided by doctrine, and seduced by the spirit of the age. To many believers looking at the headlines, it can seem as if the devil has not only stormed the walls but taken up residence in the sanctuary itself. This book begins from a simple, sobering conviction: the enemy of souls has never ceased his work, and in this generation, he has directed particular fury against the historic institutions of the Christian faith.

The purpose of these pages is not to regurgitate gossip or to delight in visible failure, but to expose a pattern of spiritual attack that Scripture has already warned about. From Genesis to Revelation, the Bible teaches that Satan's preferred battleground is not the pagan temple but the people of God. The serpent slithers into Eden, not into the wilderness; Judas walks among the Twelve, not the Pharisees; wolves arise in sheep's clothing, not open persecution. The New Testament prepares believers for an uncomfortable reality: the Church's greatest wounds often come from betrayal within, false shepherds, corrupted doctrine, and hidden sin in high places.

The modern crises that have torn through the Roman Catholic Church and the Anglican Communion must be read in this light. The molestation scandals, the tolerated culture of sexual immorality within segments of the priesthood, the normalization of homosexual practice and relationships among clergy, the ordination of women and practicing homosexuals as bishops, and the wholesale revision of Christian teaching on sex and marriage are not random, isolated developments. They are symptoms of a deeper conflict, a spiritual war in which the devil aims to destroy credibility, confuse doctrine, and persuade the world that the Church is no different from any other failing human institution.

This book argues that what many describe merely as "institutional breakdown" or "cultural adaptation" is, at root, a manifestation of spiritual warfare against the very heart of Christian witness. When the Church ceases to proclaim the whole counsel of God regarding sin, repentance, and holiness, especially in the realm of sexuality, it does not become kinder or more enlightened; it becomes vulnerable. The ancient enemy is patient. He does not need to abolish the Church; he only needs to make her indistinguishable from the world she is called to save. Where there should be a prophetic voice, he prefers a timid echo. Where there should be purity, he fosters secrecy. Where there should be unity in truth, he sows factions under the banner of progress or tradition.

The author of this book has seen that war from unusual vantage points. Growing up in England and educated in private schools, he first encountered the Church not as an abstraction but as a living, imperfect community woven into the fabric of national life. His early adulthood took a very different path: joining the Coldstream Guards, followed by duty with the City of London Police, instilled in him a deep respect for discipline, hierarchy, and the harsh realities of human sin. Guarding institutions, upholding order, and confronting wrongdoing were not theoretical ideas but daily responsibilities.

Later, after relocation to the United States another chapter opened: a career in investigation and counter-intelligence, where deception, infiltration, and hidden agendas were no longer metaphors but operational realities. In that world, one learns that the most dangerous enemy is not the one shouting at the gates but the one who has quietly obtained a badge, a uniform, or a keycard. It was in this season when the techniques of subversion were part of his professional vocabulary, that God's call became louder than ever before. The skills once used to detect and resist human adversaries would be redirected toward discerning and confronting a more ancient foe.

For the last thirty years, the author has served as Anglican clergy within the Continuing Anglican movement, committed to preserving classical Anglican faith and order in the midst of widespread ecclesial compromise. Those decades have brought him into close contact with the struggles of ordinary believers trying to reconcile what they see in Scripture with what they see in their churches, and with the pain of clergy and laity who feel betrayed by leaders, synods, and denominations that they once trusted. He has stood at altars, bedsides, and gravesides; he has heard confessions, preached repentance, and watched as churches fracture under the pressure of doctrinal and moral upheaval.

His own household reflects both the cost and the calling of service. He is married to Melissa, a United States Marine combat veteran, who was forcibly medically retired after 26 years of service; whose courage and endurance have been forged in a different kind of conflict. Together they have raised three children to adulthood; two of them now serve as Marines themselves and the eldest is in the performing arts in California. In their family life, military duty, sacrifice, and spiritual vocation intertwine. The language of warfare, duty, loyalty, courage, vigilance is not mere rhetoric but a lived experience. It is from this union of martial discipline and pastoral responsibility that the author writes about the warfare of the Church.

These personal details are not offered to center a personality, but to make clear that the argument of this book is shaped both by Scripture and by encounters with real forms of conflict, political, institutional, and spiritual. Any military service member knows that an undefended gate is an invitation; an investigator knows that a pattern of silence hides deeper secrets; a priest knows that unconfessed sin eventually bears bitter fruit. When such patterns emerge in the life of the Church on a global scale, they must not be dismissed as mere coincidence, nor explained away as "the price of modernization and being contemporary." They are signals that an enemy is at work.

Therefore, this book will examine, in biblical context, how evil has attacked the two largest and most historically influential Christian communions in the West: Roman Catholicism and Anglicanism. It will trace how the devil has exploited structural weaknesses, moral failings, and cultural pressures to undermine their witness. It will explore how sexual abuse and homosexuality have ravaged trust within the Catholic priesthood, and how homosexual ordinations, the gay agenda, and the ordination of women have fractured Anglican identity and doctrine. It will also ask how these specific wounds fit into the larger pattern of spiritual deception warned about by the apostles.

Yet this is not a book of despair. To say that the serpent is in the sanctuary is not to say that Christ has abandoned His Bride. On the contrary, Scripture teaches that God often purifies His people through judgment, exposure, and crisis. The same Lord who warned that wolves would arise among the flock also promised to be with His Church to the end of the age. The aim here is not to invite cynicism but to call for discernment, repentance, and renewed courage. If the devil is indeed active each day against the Christian religion, then passive resignation is not an option.

The chapters that follow seek to help believers see with clearer eyes: to recognize the enemy's strategies, to understand how they have played out in Rome and Canterbury, and to rediscover the weapons God has provided for this very hour. Readers are invited to lay aside both naïve optimism and bitter disillusionment and instead to stand where soldiers, investigators, and pastors must all eventually stand, awake, sober, and ready, trusting that the conflict is real, the danger is great, but the victory has already been secured in Christ.

It is not unexpected that this book will be attacked by those who subscribe to the evil agenda and this may even extend to the author and his community of faithful Christians in the Conservative Anglican Communion. We therefore ask that all Christian readers pray for all involved in building the true church and protecting those who are part of it.

In history many have sacrificed their lives for the church, today we fight against a world that sacrifices the church for their lifestyle.

Chapter 1

The Ancient Enemy: A Biblical Portrait of the Devil

The seriousness of the Church's present crisis cannot be understood unless the Church first recovers a sober, biblical understanding of her enemy. Modern Western Christianity often speaks easily of "broken systems," "poor leadership," or "changing cultures," but hesitates to speak plainly of the devil. Yet Scripture does not share that reluctance. From the opening chapters of Genesis to the closing visions of Revelation, it presents a personal, intelligent adversary who relentlessly opposes God's purposes and the people who bear His name. If the Church forgets this, she will inevitably misread her troubles and misdiagnose her wounds.

The Bible's first introduction to Satan is indirect, but unmistakable. In Genesis, the serpent appears in the Garden not as a mythic symbol of generic evil, but as a speaking, reasoning tempter who questions God's Word and character. He does not attack Adam and Eve with violence; he attacks them with suggestion. "Did God really say…?" is his opening gambit, and it has echoed through every age of the Church. His initial success rests on three moves that will define his method forever: he casts doubt on the truth of God's command, he downplays the seriousness of disobedience, and he offers an alternative vision of goodness and fulfillment apart from God. The fall of humanity begins not with a sword, but with a conversation.

Later, in the book of Job, the veil is pulled back further. Satan appears not as a free agent roaming the cosmos at will, but as a rebel spirit who still comes before God's throne to accuse the righteous. He challenges Job's integrity and insinuates that faithfulness is nothing more than self-interest: remove the blessings, he argues, and the believer will curse God to His face. Here the devil is not merely a tempter but an accuser, seeking permission to test, afflict, and destroy. The suffering that follows is not random tragedy; it is a calculated attempt to sever the bond between God and His servant by means of pain, loss, and confusion. Job's story reveals another constant of spiritual warfare: Satan desires to use adversity not simply to harm bodies and possessions, but to poison trust.

By the time the New Testament opens, the enemy's identity and intent are unmistakable. In the wilderness, the devil confronts Christ Himself. Again, he does not begin with overt hostility; he begins with Scripture. He quotes the Word of God while twisting its meaning, offering Jesus a kingdom without a cross, glory without obedience, and authority without submission to the Father. Here the pattern seen in Eden reaches its sharpest point: Satan will always be content for people to speak of God, of Scripture, even of Christ Himself, so long as the truth is bent just enough to serve rebellion. He is at his most dangerous not when he denies the Bible outright, but when he misuses it in the service of disobedience.

Jesus does not treat the devil as metaphor or parable. He

speaks of him as "the ruler of this world," "a murderer from the beginning," and "the father of lies." Christ's exorcisms are not theatrical embellishments but visible signs that a stronger man has come to bind the strong man and plunder his house. The Gospels show that wherever the kingdom of God advances, demonic resistance intensifies. The presence of the Son exposes and enrages the prince of darkness, and the clash becomes visible in tormented souls, unclean spirits, and the open opposition of religious leaders who unknowingly align themselves with the adversary's purposes.

The devil's tactics, however, are not limited to pagan villages or obviously possessed individuals. One of the most sobering scenes in the New Testament occurs when Jesus predicts His passion and Peter, out of misplaced zeal and love, rebukes Him. Christ's response is swift and chilling: "Get behind me, Satan." Here is a beloved disciple, a future apostle, momentarily speaking under the influence of a mindset that would divert the Messiah from His cross. This does not mean Peter is demon-possessed or consciously malicious. It means that Satan is quite willing to exploit sincere but misguided believers, especially when they are trying to steer Christ, and later, Christ's Church, away from the path of costly obedience.

The betrayal by Judas escalates this reality. The Gospels state that "Satan entered into Judas," and through his treachery, the Lord of glory is delivered into the hands of His enemies. It is crucial to notice where this takes place: not among the Pharisees, not on Rome's benches, but at Christ's own table. The devil's hand reaches into the inner circle. The lesson is unavoidable: proximity to holy things, office among the people of God, even participation in the visible company of the apostles, is no guarantee against satanic influence when the heart is covetous, embittered, or unbelieving.

The rest of the New Testament echoes this sober awareness. The apostle Paul warns that Satan disguises himself as an angel of light, and that his servants may appear as servants of righteousness. That means evil often comes to the Church baptized in respectable language, clothed in religious office, and carrying credentials that command trust. False apostles, deceitful workers, and teachers of a different gospel do not introduce themselves as agents of the enemy. They present themselves as enlightened reformers, compassionate pastors, or sophisticated theologians. Their danger lies precisely in their plausibility.

Paul also speaks of "the schemes of the devil" and commands believers to put on the whole armor of God. Schemes imply strategy, long-term, adaptable, tailored to the weaknesses of a particular people at a particular time. The enemy is not merely reactive; he is proactive, studying the Church's vulnerabilities, probing for cracks in doctrine, discipline, and devotion. Where he finds pride, he whispers flattery. Where he finds fear, he offers compromise. Where he finds weariness, he suggests doctrinal shortcuts and moral exceptions. His warfare is patient, cumulative, and often generational.

The letters of Peter and John add yet another dimension.

Peter describes the devil as a roaring lion, seeking someone to devour. John speaks of "the whole world lying in the power of the evil one" and warns of antichrists who arise from within the community of believers. These antichrists do not necessarily deny Christ with their lips; they may redefine Him, strip Him of His authority, or recast Him as a mere moral teacher whose words must be updated to suit modern sensibilities. The spirit of antichrist is the spirit of substitution: another Christ, another gospel, another standard of holiness, all presented as progress or deeper insight.

The book of Revelation finally pulls the threads together. Satan appears as the great dragon, the ancient serpent, the deceiver of the whole world, and the accuser of the brethren. He persecutes the Church externally through beastly empires and seduces her internally through false prophets and seductive harlots. The imagery is dramatic, but the realities are familiar: political pressure, cultural seduction, and religious deception form a threefold cord of attack. The dragon's hatred of the woman and her offspring, symbolic of the Church reveals his unrelenting focus: to destroy faith, corrupt worship, and silence testimony.

Gathering these biblical strands, a coherent portrait emerges. Satan is a personal, intelligent, and malicious being who:

- Questions and twists God's Word.

- Accuses the people of God before God and before their own consciences.

- Seeks to infiltrate the closest circles of spiritual authority.

- Prefers disguise to open display, often appearing as light, wisdom, or compassion.

- Uses suffering, shame, and scandal to drive believers into despair and unbelief.

- Exploits culture, power, and religious structures as instruments of deception.

This portrait must shape how the Church interprets her present condition. If the devil is real and if his tactics are consistent, then the moral collapse of clergy, the spread of false doctrine, the public disgrace of institutions, and the internal division of communions cannot be understood merely as human error or unfortunate coincidence. They must be seen as part of a broader, coordinated assault on the credibility and holiness of the people of God. The fact that bishops wear miters, priests don vestments, and theologians occupy endowed chairs does not place them beyond the reach of these strategies; in many ways, it makes them prime targets.

At the same time, this biblical picture guards against both naïve optimism and paranoid obsession. The Church is not called to see demons behind every difficulty, nor to absolve human responsibility by blaming every sin on the devil. Scripture always holds together two truths: Satan is active, and human beings are accountable. The devil can tempt, deceive, and accuse; he cannot force obedience. When leaders fall, when communions compromise, when doctrines are diluted, there is always a human choice involved, fear of man over fear of God, comfort over faithfulness, reputation over repentance. Spiritual warfare does not excuse sin; it reveals the stakes of sin.

Recovering a biblical portrait of the devil also restores the Church's confidence in God's sovereignty. The book of Job, the temptation of Christ, and the visions of Revelation all affirm that Satan operates on a leash. He is powerful but not ultimate, malicious but not sovereign. His attacks are permitted, limited, and ultimately overruled for the refinement of God's people and the display of divine glory. This does not lessen the grief of scandal or the horror of betrayal, but it does prevent despair. The enemy is dangerous yet defeated; active, yet doomed.

This first chapter, then, lays the foundation for everything that follows. Before examining Rome's scandals or Canterbury's capitulations, the Church must be reminded that she has an adversary who has been perfecting his craft since Eden. The same voice that whispered, "Did God really say?" in the Garden now whispers in synods, seminaries, and chanceries. The same spirit that entered Judas now seeks willing hosts in clergy who cherish secret sin or ambition above obedience. The same deceiver who offered Christ a crossless kingdom now offers churches a costless discipleship and a gospel without repentance.

If the Church is to understand how the devil has attacked

Roman Catholicism and Anglicanism in particular, she must begin here, with clear eyes on the ancient enemy, his character, and his methods. Only then can she recognize his fingerprints on modern events, resist his lies with confidence, and cling more firmly to the One who came "to destroy the works of the devil."

Chapter 2

The Church as the Target of Hell

From the moment Christ declared, "I will build my Church, and the gates of hell shall not prevail against it," the battlefield was clearly defined. The Church is not an accidental bystander in history's spiritual conflict; she is its central target. Hell does not waste time attacking what does not matter. The very existence of a visible, organized, sacramental people bearing Christ's name and entrusted with His Word makes the Church a primary objective for the enemy of souls. To understand why evil has pressed so fiercely against Roman Catholicism and Anglicanism in particular, the Church must first grasp why she herself stands at the center of Satan's strategy.

The New Testament presents the Church as both fragile and indestructible. She is fragile because she is composed of sinners still capable of falling, betraying, and wandering. She is indestructible because she is founded on Christ, who cannot be shaken. This paradox explains why the devil does not attempt to topple Christ from His throne; it is an impossible task, but instead aims to disfigure Christ's Body on earth. If the evil one cannot dethrone the Head, he will discredit the Bride. The strategy is simple and devastating, corrupt her leaders, confuse her doctrine, fracture her unity, and stain her witness before the watching world.

Christ Himself warned that the Church's greatest threats would arise from within. He spoke of wolves in sheep's clothing, inwardly ravenous while outwardly pious. These wolves do not prowl outside the flock; they dwell among it, feed upon it, and often guide it. The apostle Paul echoed this warning when he told the Ephesian elders that from among their own number men would arise speaking twisted things to draw disciples after themselves. The danger does not come only from atheistic philosophers, pagan rulers, or hostile cultures. It comes from pastors, bishops, theologians, and teachers who bear Christian titles while undermining Christian truth.

This internal vulnerability has been evident throughout the Church's history. In the early centuries, heresies rarely emerged from complete outsiders; they sprang up from bishops, priests, monks, and learned men who enjoyed respect and influence. Arianism, which denied the full divinity of Christ, did not arise from the streets but from within episcopal circles. Pelagianism, which minimized the necessity of grace, came from a monk engaged in moral exhortation. Time and again, the Church's gravest doctrinal crises began with someone inside the walls offering a "better," "more reasonable," or "more compassionate" version of the faith. These movements did not announce themselves as betrayals; they presented themselves as developments.

The devil's logic in targeting the Church is ruthlessly efficient. If he can corrupt a single prominent teacher, he can mislead thousands. If he can compromise a bishop or a priest, he can shake the faith of entire parishes and dioceses. If he can infiltrate seminaries, he can shape the next generation of clergy according to his lies. A single scandal in the life of a well-known leader can do more to discredit the Gospel in the eyes of skeptics than a thousand arguments. Spiritual warfare at the institutional level is therefore highly leveraged: the enemy concentrates his effort where the damage will be greatest and the fallout widest.

At the same time, Satan's targeting of the Church is not limited to moral corruption. He also wages war through doctrinal confusion. The apostles repeatedly warned that in the latter days people would not endure sound teaching but would accumulate teachers to suit their own desires. This falling away does not appear overnight; it emerges gradually as churches soften unpopular doctrines, downplay the demands of holiness, and reinterpret Scripture to align with the spirit of the age. False teaching is rarely advertised as such. The popularity of the Prosperity Gospel is one such example. It usually enters under the banners of nuance, progress, or contextualization, all while subtly relocating authority from God's Word to human preference.

The visible unity of the Church is another of hell's chosen targets. Christ prayed that His followers would be one so that the world might believe the Father sent Him. Division therefore strikes at the heart of the Church's mission. The enemy exploits pride, cultural differences, personal grievances, and theological disputes to fracture communion. Schisms and splintering may begin over legitimate concerns, but once charity and humility are lost, the devil rejoices. A divided Church presents a distorted image of Christ to the world: instead of a single Body, there appears a marketplace of competing brands, each claiming authenticity.

Yet the assault is not purely structural or doctrinal. It is also sacramental and pastoral. When the devil infiltrates the Church, he aims to rob her sacraments of credibility and her shepherds of trust. If those who administer baptism, preach the Word, and celebrate the Eucharist are exposed as liars, predators, or apostates, the faithful are tempted to doubt not only the ministers, but the mysteries themselves. Children raised in such environments may abandon the faith entirely, unable to separate the holy things of God from the unholy behavior of those who handled them. In this way, the enemy's attack on the Church becomes an attack on generations.

None of this means the Church is merely a passive victim. Scripture insists that judgment begins with the household of God. When the Church tolerates sin, refuses correction, or silences whistleblowers, she cooperates with her adversary. When leaders prioritize institutional reputation over truth, or political alliances over fidelity, they open doors to infiltration. Hell may be the architect of certain schemes, but human beings build and furnish the rooms. Recognizing that the Church is a target must never become an excuse; it must become a summons to vigilance and repentance.

It is also essential to remember that the devil's targeting of the Church is a backhanded tribute to her importance. He does not wage such effort against what is irrelevant. The sacraments he seeks to profane are real; the doctrines he twists are true; the souls he tries to devour are precious. If the Church were just another human association, the enemy would not fear her or bother with her. His fury is precisely because Christ has entrusted her with the Gospel, the means of grace, and the keys of the kingdom. Attacking her is his way of striking at God's plan for the salvation of the world.

In light of this, believers must learn to interpret the crises of Roman Catholicism and Anglicanism not simply as institutional embarrassments, but as battlegrounds. When bishops conceal abuse to "protect the Church," they have already forgotten that the Church's true beauty lies in holiness, not image management. When synods update doctrine to match cultural norms, they have already surrendered the field of truth. The enemy has no difficulty working with either conservative hypocrisy or liberal apostasy; his only concern is to obscure Christ.

This chapter's purpose is to establish the Church's place in the enemy's line of fire so that the case studies to follow are seen in their true light. The scandals of Rome and the capitulations of Canterbury are not isolated failures of two unrelated institutions. They are episodes in a single war. The same adversary who whispered in Eden and tempted Christ in the wilderness now whispers in chanceries, assemblies, and theological faculties. The same strategy, distort the Word, seduce the leaders, scatter the flock, plays out in different guises across centuries.

Before turning to those specific stories, the Church must acknowledge a hard truth: to be the Body of Christ in history is to live under fire. There is no neutral ground, no safe institutional height above the fray. Every parish, every diocese, every communion is either resisting or accommodating the enemy's designs. Once this is understood, the shocking events of recent decades no longer appear as inexplicable anomalies. They become recognizable as what they have always been: targeted strikes against the very heart of Christian witness.

Chapter 3

Rome Under Siege: Scandal and Shame in the Priesthood

The crisis that erupted within the Roman Catholic Church at the close of the twentieth century and into the twenty-first did not begin with headlines. It began in quiet rooms, concealed files, whispered warnings, and long-suppressed testimonies. For decades, children, adolescents, and vulnerable adults suffered abuse at the hands of men ordained to represent Christ and entrusted with the care of souls. In many places, their cries were minimized, dismissed, or buried beneath layers of institutional instinct and legal maneuvering. When the truth finally broke into public view, it shocked not only Catholics but the world. The priest, who should have been an icon of holiness, was suddenly associated in the public mind with predation and betrayal. Rome, long viewed as the bulwark of moral teaching, found herself exposed as a house with rotting beams.

From a merely sociological perspective, the scandal can be described in terms of systemic failure: flawed seminary formation, clericalism, inadequate oversight, and a culture of secrecy. Those factors are real and must be faced honestly. Yet if the Church is what she claims to be; a visible instrument of Christ's saving work, then this catastrophe cannot be explained adequately without recognizing the hand of a personal enemy. The devil delights in turning God's gifts into weapons against His people. There are few strategies more effective than corrupting those who stand at the altar, hear confessions, and proclaim the Gospel. When a priest abuses, the sacrilege is double: the victim's dignity is attacked, and God's own name is dragged through the mud.

Scripture offers sobering parallels. In the days of Eli, his sons, also priests were described as "worthless men" who abused their office, exploited the people, and lay with women who served at the entrance of the tent of meeting. Their sins brought judgment not only on themselves but on the entire house, and ultimately on Israel's sanctuary. The Old Testament does not treat such misconduct as private moral failure; it presents it as a desecration that pollutes the worship of the people and invites divine wrath. In like manner, the sexual crimes and corrupt lifestyles of some Catholic clergy have not been merely "personal weaknesses." They have wounded the Body of Christ, scandalized the little ones, and contributed to a profound crisis of faith for countless souls.

The pattern of institutional response intensified the damage. In too many cases, those responsible for oversight responded not as shepherds but as managers. Rather than bringing sin into the light, they moved offenders to new assignments, relied on therapeutic assurances, or framed the problem as a public relations risk to be contained. This instinct, to protect the image of the Church rather than the integrity of the flock played directly into the enemy's hands. The devil is not only a tempter; he is an accuser. Every act of concealment furnished him with more material. Every quiet transfer, every threatened victim, every ignored complaint ensured that when exposure finally came, it would explode with maximal force.

The effects on the faithful were devastating. In parish after parish, believers discovered that the priest they trusted, the bishop they respected, or the diocese they assumed to be safe had been part of a chain of silence. Many victims abandoned the faith altogether, unable to endure the thought of drawing near to a God whose representatives had harmed them. Others remained but did so with a mixture of grief, anger, and suspicion. Parents looked at clergy with a new wariness. Young men who once might have considered a vocation now hesitated, fearing association with a disgraced institution. Vocations declined, donations dropped, and the moral authority of Rome on questions of sexuality and family life was gravely weakened.

From the perspective of spiritual warfare, this is precisely the outcome the devil seeks. If he can persuade the world that the Church's claim to holiness is a lie, he can hinder many from ever hearing the Gospel with an open heart. When the same institution that condemns sexual sin is revealed to have harbored and shuffled abusers, its teaching appears hypocritical and self-serving. Even where the doctrine remains true, its human messengers have been compromised. The result is a powerful temptation: to conclude that if priests and bishops do not believe or live what they teach, then the teaching itself must be false or irrelevant. Cynicism becomes a shield against conversion.

It is important, however, to see that this catastrophe did not occur in a vacuum. The enemy exploited existing weaknesses within the Roman system. Clericalism, the exaggerated elevation of clergy above laity created a culture in which priests were often treated as untouchable, their word privileged above all others. A vow of celibacy, rightly lived, is a powerful sign of total devotion to Christ. Wrongly formed and poorly supervised, it can also become a cover for immaturity, unresolved disordered desires, or hidden double lives. A hierarchical structure, designed to provide unity and order, can be twisted into a mechanism for suppressing bad news. Such features are not evil in themselves, but they become vulnerable points when humility, transparency, and genuine accountability are lacking.

The presence of homosexual subcultures within seminaries and clergy networks further complicated matters. When groups of priests share not only a calling but a shared pattern of secret sin, mutual compromise becomes a form of protection. The one who would otherwise call another to repentance finds his own conscience bound by fear of exposure. In that environment, the devil gains a foothold not only in individual hearts but in relationships, making it costly to speak truth and easy to rationalize silence. What may have begun as personal weakness becomes, over time, a web of complicity.

None of this absolves individuals of responsibility. Each abuser, each enabling superior, each official who chose image over integrity will answer to God for those decisions. But the scale and depth of the crisis reveal more than the sum of personal sins. They reveal a targeted assault on the priesthood itself. If the priest is called to resemble Christ the Good Shepherd, then corrupting priests is a way of smearing the face of Christ before the world. If the confessional is meant to be a place of healing, turning it into a site of violation is a way of mocking the very idea of mercy. In this sense, the scandal is not only a tragedy; it is blasphemy in action.

And yet, amid the ruins, there are signs of grace. Survivors who have found the courage to tell their stories have brought hidden darkness into the light. Faithful priests and laypeople who refused to accept the old patterns have called their leaders to account. Reforms, however imperfect, have begun to change how accusations are handled, how seminarians are formed, and how oversight is exercised. These developments do not erase the evil done, but they bear witness to a truth deeper than the scandal: the Holy Spirit has not abandoned the Church, and Christ still walks among the lampstands, exposing, cleansing, and judging.

For Rome, the path forward will require more than policies and protocols. It will require a renewed embrace of holiness as the true badge of authority, a rejection of clerical privilege that treats priests as a protected caste, and a willingness to endure the humiliation of continued exposure rather than return to the false safety of secrecy. The devil has had his hour in many chanceries and rectories, but his triumph need not be final. If bishops and priests will humble themselves, confess, and truly reform, what the enemy intended for destruction can become, in

God's providence, a painful but purifying fire.

This chapter has examined how the sexual abuse crisis in the Roman Catholic Church manifests the enemy's strategy: infiltrate the ranks of leadership, exploit structural weaknesses, weaponize secrecy, and then unleash scandal to discredit the Church's witness. In the chapters to come, a parallel story will be traced in another great communion, the Anglican world, where the attack has taken a somewhat different form. If Rome's wound has been exposed chiefly through abuse and cover-up, Anglicanism's has been revealed through doctrinal capitulation and moral revision. In both cases, however, the root issue is the same: the Church as the chosen target of hell, and the urgent need for discernment, repentance, and courage in the midst of war.

Chapter 4

The Spirit of Perversion: Homosexuality and the Priesthood

The sexual abuse scandals that shook the Roman Catholic Church exposed, at their core, the violation of the weak by those who vowed to protect them. Yet behind the horrific pattern of abuse and cover-up lies another, more subtle deformation: a culture in which disordered sexual desires and practices were tolerated, normalized, or quietly excused among those entrusted with sacred office. This chapter does not attempt to equate every instance of homosexual inclination with abuse, nor to deny that heterosexual sin also stains the priesthood. Rather, it seeks to show how a tolerated pattern of homosexual practice and subculture within clerical life opened a door for the enemy to distort the priestly vocation, compromise moral clarity, and weaken the Church's witness on matters of sexuality and holiness.

From a biblical standpoint, the issue at stake is not the singling out of one sin as uniquely damning, but the recognition that sexual conduct precisely because it touches the body, covenant, and identity has profound spiritual implications. Scripture consistently teaches that sexual immorality, of whatever kind, defiles the temple of the Holy Spirit and contradicts God's design for human flourishing. It presents marriage as the union of man and woman, ordered toward mutual love, procreation, and the reflection of Christ and His Church. Any persistent pattern that departs from this design, whether heterosexual or homosexual, is not merely a private matter; it is a rejection of the Creator's wisdom. When such patterns are present among clergy, the contradiction becomes sharper still, because their lives are meant to be living icons of the Gospel they proclaim.

The priest, especially in the Latin tradition, is called to a life of celibacy. Properly understood, celibacy is not a denial of sexuality but an offering of it to God, an undivided devotion that becomes a sign of the kingdom where "they neither marry nor are given in marriage." The celibate priest is meant to remind the Church that her ultimate Bridegroom is Christ, and that the deepest hunger of the human heart is satisfied not in any earthly union but in communion with God. When embraced freely, joyfully, and with the support of sound formation, celibacy can be a luminous witness to heaven's reality.

Yet celibacy, like any powerful sign, can be distorted. When seminarians are poorly formed, left emotionally immature, or encouraged to treat vows as mere formalities, the gap between the ideal and the lived reality can become a breeding ground for hypocrisy. In such an environment, men with unresolved same-sex desires may enter the priesthood for complex reasons: a desire to escape scrutiny, an unconscious hope that celibacy will "fix" them, or even the perception that clerical life offers a socially acceptable space to avoid heterosexual marriage. If the seminary and diocesan culture then tolerates, or even quietly fosters, active homosexual subcultures, celibacy becomes a fiction.

The outward form remains, but the inward reality is hollowed out.

Where homosexual networks are established within the clergy, they often operate with an internal logic of mutual protection. Members know one another's secrets; they share vulnerabilities that can be used, if necessary, to ensure loyalty and silence. In such a setting, the normal mechanisms of fraternal correction and discipline are weakened. A priest who might otherwise call a brother to repentance hesitates, knowing that his own compromised life could be exposed in return. The fear of scandal, understood here as exposure, not sin becomes a governing principle. Over time, this shared vulnerability can evolve into a culture of tacit permission: so long as indiscretions remain discreet, they will be overlooked.

The devil is a strategist, not a mere opportunist. A priesthood marked by secret sexual disorder offers him multiple advantages. First, it erodes personal holiness. A man who habitually lives a double life cannot preach with full authority about chastity, marriage, or self-denial; his conscience knows the distance between pulpit and practice. Second, it compromises doctrinal integrity. Clergy who are deeply entangled in homosexual practice or ideology will naturally resist clear, biblical teaching on sexuality. They may downplay or reinterpret the Church's doctrine, recasting it as harsh or outdated, while presenting their revisionist stance as compassionate and pastoral. Third, it weakens institutional resolve. Bishops who know, or strongly suspect, the private lives of their priests may avoid firm action out of fear that a chain of revelation will implicate others or themselves.

As this culture deepens, the message communicated to seminarians and younger clergy is unmistakable: whatever the Catechism may say, "real life" in the rectory operates by different rules. Slogans about love, accompaniment, and inclusion can be co-opted to justify moral laxity, while those who seek to live celibate chastity are made to feel naïve, rigid, or "repressed." In some places, men who openly affirm the Church's teaching on homosexuality and chastity find themselves marginalized, mocked, or quietly sidelined, while those aligned with a more permissive ethos rise in influence. The enemy delights in such inversions. The virtues he most fears, obedience, purity, and truth-telling are cast as vices, while the vices he foments present themselves as enlightened mercy.

It must be repeated that homosexual inclination, in itself, is not a sin, and that men who experience such attractions yet strive sincerely to live in chastity and obedience are not the problem this chapter addresses. The Church has always called all believers, regardless of particular temptations, to holiness, and many who carry this cross do so heroically. The focus here is on a structural and cultural phenomenon: the emergence and toleration of active homosexual networks, the protection of clergy living in unrepentant sexual relationships, and the resultant distortion of both pastoral care and doctrinal teaching. Where this occurs, the priesthood ceases to be a visible sign of the kingdom's purity and becomes instead a compromised caste, more concerned with maintaining an internal peace than with conforming to the mind of Christ.

At the spiritual level, this represents a perversion of vocation. The priest is called to be a spiritual father, imaging the love of God the Father for His children. Fatherhood, whether natural or spiritual, is characterized by self-gift, protection, and fruitful responsibility. When a priest's sexual life, whether in thought, fantasy, or action is turned inward and distorted, his ability to exercise authentic fatherhood is impaired. The enemy's goal is not only to trap the priest in sin, but to render him sterile in ministry: unable to generate life through preaching, sacraments, and example because his own life is divided and compromised.

Furthermore, the presence of a visible homosexual culture within the clergy creates confusion among the faithful. Ordinary Catholics, especially younger generations, see or hear of priests who publicly support same-sex relationships, attend or bless same-sex unions, or openly dissent from the Church's teaching on these matters, yet face little or no consequence. The signal is clear: the Church's doctrine is optional, a kind of ideal for the books while "real" pastoral practice moves in a different direction. This disconnect between official teaching and tolerated practice is one of the enemy's most effective tools for undermining confidence in truth itself. If doctrine is merely aspirational rhetoric, then conscience becomes the final arbiter, and the Church loses her prophetic voice.

In addition, the broader culture's aggressive promotion of the LGBT agenda has placed enormous pressure on the Church. Media narratives, legal frameworks, and educational systems routinely present homosexual behavior and identity as not only acceptable but morally superior expressions of authenticity and love. In such a climate, bishops and priests are tempted to soften their stance, avoid "controversial" topics, or adopt ambiguous language that can be heard one way by the faithful and another by the world. The enemy's tactic here is subtle: he does not always demand explicit denial of doctrine; he often settles for a silence that speaks loudly, a vagueness that permits error to flourish unchecked.

What then is the path of resistance? It begins where all Christian renewal must begin with truth and repentance. The Church must speak clearly about sexual morality, including homosexual acts, not as a matter of culture war, but as a matter of fidelity to God's revelation and concern for souls. Bishops and superiors must insist that those preparing for priesthood accept, internalize, and seek to live the Church's teaching in its fullness. Where there is evidence of entrenched homosexual subcultures or networks, decisive action is needed, not as a witch hunt, but as a necessary purification of the priestly state. Mercy for individuals can never mean complicity with structures of sin.

At the same time, the Church must provide robust, honest formation in chastity, emotional maturity, and friendship. Seminarians and priests who experience same-sex attraction should not be driven into secrecy, where the devil thrives, but invited into an environment where they can receive support, guidance, and accountability in living celibate fidelity. The aim is not to create a class of ostracized strugglers, but to form men whose weakness becomes a place of grace, not a secret gateway for the enemy. Transparency and spiritual accompaniment are crucial; isolation is dangerous.

Finally, the faithful must learn to distinguish between the office and the man. The failure, hypocrisy, or disordered life of a priest does not invalidate the sacraments he celebrates nor nullify the truths he may still preach. Christ remains the true High Priest, and His grace is not bound by the unworthiness of His ministers. Yet acknowledging this must not become an excuse for lowered expectations. On the contrary, it should intensify the Church's insistence that those who bear the indelible mark of Holy Orders strive for purity of heart and body, knowing how high a trust has been placed in them.

The spirit of perversion that has entangled portions of the priesthood is not invincible. It feeds on secrecy, self-deception, and institutional cowardice. Wherever truth is spoken, sin confessed, victims honored, and genuine reform embraced, that spirit is driven back. The devil has worked hard to turn the priestly state into a place of scandal and confusion; God intends it to be a sign of the kingdom's holiness. The contest between these two realities is far from over. In the chapters ahead, the focus will shift from Rome to Canterbury, where a different but related drama has unfolded: not primarily hidden networks of sin, but public redefinitions of doctrine and the reordering of ministry itself under the banner of inclusion and progress.

Chapter 5

The Fall of the Anglican Church: When Orthodoxy Collapsed

The story of Anglicanism in the last century is, in many ways, a slow-motion spiritual landslide. From a distance, the changes can appear as a series of discrete decisions: revisions to liturgy, new methods of biblical interpretation, the ordination of women, the consecration of openly homosexual bishops, and the blessing of same-sex unions. Each step was often defended as pastoral, compassionate, or necessary for relevance in a changing world. Yet when viewed together, these developments reveal a deeper and more troubling reality: a communion slowly trading revealed truth for cultural approval, biblical authority for human sentiment, and catholic order for ideological experimentation. The visible Anglican world did not collapse overnight; it eroded over decades, as the foundations of orthodoxy were quietly chipped away.

To understand how this happened, one must look back to the rise of theological liberalism in the nineteenth and twentieth centuries. In universities and seminaries, new methods of biblical criticism began to treat Scripture less as the authoritative Word of God and more as a human record of religious experience. Miracles were questioned, moral norms were reinterpreted, and doctrines once considered non-negotiable were recast as products of their time. Within Anglicanism, this spirit of revision found a ready home in certain quarters: the desire to be intellectually respectable in the eyes of the academia made many leaders receptive to ideas that subtly undermined confidence in the plain teaching of the Bible. Once Scripture is no longer the final court of appeal, every doctrine, including those on sex and ministry, becomes vulnerable to renegotiation.

The first major visible crack appeared in the debate over women's ordination. For centuries, Anglicanism, like the rest of historic Christendom had restricted priestly and episcopal orders to men, seeing this not as a statement of inferiority, but as faithfulness to the pattern given by Christ and the apostles. When the push arose to ordain women, the argument was framed largely in terms of justice, equality, and the gifts of women. Opponents appealed to Scripture, tradition, and the symbolic nuptial meaning of the priest as icon of Christ the Bridegroom. Proponents countered that such arguments were culturally conditioned and that the Spirit was "doing a new thing." In many provinces, the innovation carried the day.

This decision was far more than a change in personnel; it marked a decisive shift in how Anglicans understood authority. When the Church feels free to alter the received pattern of holy orders against the united witness of Scripture and the universal practice of East and West, it implicitly declares that contemporary convictions can override catholic consensus. Once that principle is accepted, the door stands open for further revisions. If the Church may reconfigure the priesthood and episcopate to accord with modern notions of equality, why should she not also reconfigure her teaching on sex, marriage, and the body to accord with modern notions of love and identity?

The next battlefields arose quickly. As Western culture embraced the sexual revolution and, later, the normalization of homosexual practice and relationships, many Anglican leaders faced intense pressure to "update" the Church's stance. Traditional teaching, grounded in Scripture and affirmed across centuries, held that sexual intimacy belonged within the covenant of marriage between one man and one woman, and that homosexual acts, like all sexual activity outside such marriage, were contrary to God's design. Increasingly, however, this view was branded as bigoted, harmful, and incompatible with the new moral order. Rather than challenge this narrative, large segments of Anglican leadership chose to adapt to it.

The consecration of openly homosexual and partnered bishops became a watershed. It was not merely that individuals who struggled with same-sex attraction were in ministry, a reality present in all communions, but that leaders were publicly and proudly living in relationships the Church had always regarded as sinful and then asking the Church to bless those unions. This move signaled a fundamental inversion: sin was redefined as identity, and identity as something God must affirm. The pastoral language of inclusion and welcome, which in its proper sense belongs to the Gospel, was harnessed to justify a rejection of biblical norms. The devil's strategy here was subtle and effective: he wrapped rebellion in the vocabulary of love.

The consequences for Anglican unity were immediate and

severe. Provinces in the Global South, where biblical faith and moral conservatism remained strong, protested that the West had abandoned the faith once delivered to the saints. Appeals for restraint, repentance, or at least delay were largely ignored. Instruments of communion, Lambeth Conferences, Primates' Meetings, and the Archbishop of Canterbury's moral authority, proved incapable of enforcing doctrinal discipline or restoring order. Declarations of "impaired communion," boycotts of international gatherings, and the formation of alternative structures followed. What had long presented itself as a single worldwide family of churches now fractured into competing alignments, each claiming the Anglican name while walking in different directions.

From the standpoint of spiritual warfare, the pattern is recognizable. First, the authority of Scripture is quietly diminished through academic skepticism and pastoral ambiguity. Second, a presenting issue, in this case, women's ordination, becomes a test of whether the Church will submit to the received order or reshape it to mirror the culture. Third, once the precedent of doctrinal and structural innovation is set, further changes follow, especially in the realm of sexuality, where fallen human desires clamor for affirmation. Fourth, the resulting division is framed not as a tragedy to be repented of, but as a necessary part of "prophetic witness" or "walking apart," cementing the schism. The enemy achieves multiple goals at once: truth is obscured, unity is shattered, and the Church's public voice is confused.

It is essential to see that many of those who championed

change within Anglicanism did not view themselves as enemies of Christ. They spoke passionately of justice, inclusion, and compassion. They invoked the language of the Spirit's leading, accused opponents of hardness of heart, and interpreted resistance as fear. This is precisely what makes the situation so perilous. The devil rarely advances by recruiting overt enemies; he prefers to enlist those convinced they are doing good. By appealing to genuine Christian instincts, mercy, concern for the marginalized, a desire to reach the lost, he can redirect them away from repentance and toward affirmation of what God forbids. The result is a counterfeit gospel in which the cross is emptied of its call to die to self, and grace is reduced to unconditional endorsement.

The impact on ordinary Anglicans has been profound. In many parishes, believers have watched as liturgies subtly shift, sermons avoid hard passages, and catechesis becomes thin or non-existent on matters of sexual ethics. Children grow up hearing conflicting messages from different clergy: some uphold historic teaching, others openly contradict it, and many remain silent. Confusion becomes the norm. Those who hold to traditional doctrine are sometimes treated as embarrassments or obstacles to progress. In some dioceses, faithful congregations have found themselves forced to choose between conscience and property, leaving historic buildings behind to maintain fidelity to the faith. The cost of resistance has been high.

Nevertheless, in the midst of this collapse, God has preserved witnesses. Continuing Anglican bodies, orthodox dioceses, and global realignment movements have arisen to maintain classical Anglican doctrine, worship, and moral teaching. These groups are far from perfect, and they too face temptations of pride, division, and reactionism. Yet their existence testifies that the Spirit has not abandoned the Anglican heritage; instead, He has called men and women out of compromised structures to preserve a faithful remnant. Where Canterbury falters, other centers of gravity have emerged, particularly in the Global South, reminding the West that the Church is larger than its most liberal provinces.

For those considering the Anglican story through the lens of spiritual warfare, several lessons become clear. First, once the Church ceases to treat Scripture as the non-negotiable Word of God, every doctrine and moral teaching becomes provisional. Second, symbolic changes that appear merely structural, such as altering the pattern of holy orders, often carry deep theological implications that unfold over time. Third, language matters: when biblical terms like love, justice, and inclusion are redefined according to secular ideologies, they can be used to smuggle in teachings utterly opposed to the Gospel. Fourth, unity built on sentiment rather than truth cannot endure; it will fragment under pressure.

The fall of Anglican orthodoxy in much of the Western world is not the final word on the Anglican tradition. But it stands as a grave warning to all communions: no church, however venerable its history, however beautiful its liturgy, is immune to deception. The enemy does not always attack with persecution; often he comes with applause, academic respectability, and the promise of being "on the right side of history." Those who accept his terms may gain temporary honor from the world, but they do so at the cost of their prophetic voice and, ultimately, their faithfulness to Christ.

In the chapters that follow, attention will turn more directly to the cultural tools the devil has used to advance these assaults, relativism, sexual liberation, and the cult of the sovereign self, and to the call for discernment and repentance that must sound in every part of the Church. Rome's scandals and Canterbury's capitulations are different faces of the same war. The question before believers is not whether the battle is real, but whether they will stand in the truth when standing becomes costly.

Chapter 6

The Devil's Cultural Tools

The enemy rarely attacks the Church with crude, obvious lies. More often, he works through the reigning ideas and assumptions of an age, bending them just enough to turn hearts away from God while convincing those same hearts that they are acting nobly. In the modern West, three powerful cultural currents have proven especially useful for this purpose: relativism, sexual liberation, and the cult of the sovereign self. Each of these movements contains partial truths and understandable longings, yet each, when absolutized, becomes an instrument by which the devil wages war against the mind and morals of Christians and their churches.

Relativism begins as a modest recognition of human limitation. People from different cultures and backgrounds see the world differently; they bring varied experiences to questions of right and wrong. This awareness can foster humility and patience. But when relativism hardens into a creed "there is no absolute truth," "what's true for you may not be true for me", it becomes a direct assault on the very idea that God has spoken definitively in Christ and in Scripture. If all moral claims are merely expressions of personal or communal preference, then the Church's proclamation of the Gospel as truth, rather than opinion, sounds arrogant or oppressive. Under this influence, many Christians begin to treat doctrines as private comforts rather than public realities, and moral teaching as suggestion rather than command.

The spirit of relativism infiltrates the Church in subtle ways. Sermons focus on "sharing perspectives" rather than declaring what God has revealed. Bible studies become exercises in "what this verse means to me" with little concern for what the text actually says. Heaven forbid they actually research the original language of the text. Controversial teachings are bracketed as "difficult" and quietly downplayed. The devil's goal here is not to persuade believers of a specific false doctrine, but to erode their confidence that any doctrine can be known with certainty. Once that confidence is gone, the door is open for every kind of compromise. A Church that no longer believes it can say "thus says the Lord" with conviction will soon find itself unable to resist the pressures of the age.

Sexual liberation, in turn, presents itself as a movement of freedom from repression, shame, and unjust restraints. It points to real abuses, cold marriages, hypocritical double standards, and cultures of silence around abuse and promises a world where desires can be expressed without fear. There is a grain of truth in its critique: Christians have sometimes spoken about sex in ways that fostered guilt without grace, or protected reputations rather than victims. But the sexual revolution went far beyond correcting errors. It rejected the very idea that sex belongs within a divinely ordered covenant of marriage between man and woman. Instead, it elevated desire itself as an authority: if two consenting adults agree, then their union is presumed good.

Within this framework, chastity appears not as a path to freedom, but as repression; lifelong fidelity seems naïve; and any boundaries on sexual expression are suspected of cruelty. The enemy uses this cultural script to make the Church's teaching on sex appear not only outdated but immoral. Young believers are catechized more by media, entertainment, and secular education than by Scripture. By the time they hear the Church's moral vision, it sounds to them like a foreign language. If pastors, fearing rejection, soften or abandon that vision, the result is predictable: the Church's moral witness collapses, and her people are left to navigate one of life's most powerful forces, sexual desire without the guardrails God provided.

The cult of the sovereign self is the third major tool. Modern culture tells each person: "You are your own project. Your identity is something you invent, not something you receive. Your happiness is the highest good, and anything that stands in its way is an obstacle to be removed." This message resonates deeply with fallen human nature. All of us, in our sin, want to be gods of our own worlds. The promise that we can define ourselves, our gender, our morality, our purpose feels like liberation from constraint. Yet it is, in reality, a burden too heavy for any creature to bear. We were made to receive our identity from the One who fashioned us; when we attempt to construct it alone, we build on sand.

In the realm of sexuality and gender, this cult of self manifests in the belief that inner feelings are ultimate. If someone experiences same-sex attraction, the culture tells them, "This is who you are; to question or restrain it is to deny your true self." If someone feels discomfort with their biological sex, the culture proclaims, "Your body is wrong; your sense of self is right; the body must yield." When such ideas seep into the Church, the biblical call to deny oneself, take up the cross, and follow Christ is reinterpreted as psychological harm. Any suggestion that desires should be disciplined, or that identity is given by God rather than constructed by the individual, is branded as hateful. Currently at the pinnacle of this is what is labeled . What could be more divisive to Christian beliefs than a suggestion that God, the ultimate creator got it wrong. Especially if we are created in his image.

In each of these cultural movements, the devil operates not by inventing entirely new lies, but by distorting genuine truths. The longing for understanding becomes relativism. The desire to correct injustice becomes sexual anarchy. The need for personal dignity becomes self-deification. This strategy is particularly effective in confusing Christians, because they sense that some critiques of past church failings are valid even as they are carried far beyond the bounds of truth. If the Church does not clearly distinguish between what in these movements reflects a rightful concern and what represents rebellion against God, she will either reject everything (and lose credibility) or accept everything (and lose her soul).

The impact of these cultural tools on Roman Catholicism and Anglicanism has been profound. In the Catholic world, relativism and sexual liberation made it harder for some leaders to speak plainly about sin, including homosexual acts and cohabitation, for fear of appearing harsh. In some seminaries and dioceses, therapists and "experts" were trusted more than Scripture and tradition to define what constitutes disorder or health. The language of accompaniment, rightly emphasizing patience and compassion, was sometimes stretched to justify leaving people in patterns of life incompatible with the Gospel. Meanwhile, the cult of self, made many clergy anxious about calling anyone to radical conversion; it felt more pastoral to affirm.

In Anglicanism, the same forces accelerated the embrace of revisionist doctrines. Relativism encouraged the view that global diversity justified radically different moral teachings under one ecclesial umbrella. Sexual liberation framed the Church's biblical stance on homosexuality as unjust discrimination. The cult of self underwrote a narrative in which "being true to oneself" became the highest virtue, and any call to conform one's desires to God's design was portrayed as cruelty. Under these pressures, large segments of Anglican leadership chose accommodation over confrontation. The enemy's cultural tools did their work: doctrines were softened, then reversed; traditionalists were marginalized; and the communion's visible unity fractured.

None of this means that culture itself is evil. Every age produces art, technology, and social insights that can serve the Kingdom when rightly ordered. The problem arises when the Church forgets her prophetic role and becomes an echo chamber for the prevailing ideas.

The early Christians adopted certain Roman structures and vocabulary but refused to worship Caesar. Likewise, the

Church today can affirm genuine concerns for justice, healing, and dignity while rejecting the godless philosophies that often carry those concerns. The devil's tactic is to blur this distinction until Christians feel that to oppose the ideology is to oppose the good it claims to promote.

How, then, should the Church respond to these cultural tools of the enemy? First, by recovering confidence in truth. God has spoken in Scripture and in Christ, and His Word is not rendered obsolete by changing fashions. We have no Bible 2.0. or an updated ten commandments. The Church must believe, and teach, that certain things are truly right or wrong, not because of majority vote or personal feeling, but because they correspond, or fail to correspond, to God's character and design. Second, by cultivating a robust, positive vision of Christian sexuality and identity. It is not enough to say "no" to cultural errors; believers need a compelling "yes" to God's plan for the body, marriage, celibacy, and personhood.

Third, by forming disciples who can live as a creative minority, neither retreating in fear nor surrendering in conformity. Such disciples understand the times, recognize the lies hidden within the culture's most attractive slogans, and respond with both conviction and compassion. They know that every human being, including those most captivated by relativism, sexual liberation, or the cult of self, is a person loved by God, called to repentance, and capable, by grace, of real transformation. Hatred and contempt serve the devil's purposes as surely as compromise does; the Church must resist both.

Finally, the Church must remember that cultural tides, however strong, are temporary. Empires rise and fall; philosophies bloom and wither. The devil uses them as long as they serve his designs and then discards them. When was the last time we saw marches in public supporting the women's liberation movement or encouragement for women to burn their bra? The Word of God, by contrast, endures forever. In every age, faithful believers have faced dominant ideas that mocked or contradicted the Gospel. Those who stood firm often did so at great cost, but their witness shaped history far more deeply than the fashions of their day. The same choice lies before the Church now. Will she allow relativism, sexual liberation, and the sovereign self to dictate her message and morals, or will she, in love, confront these idols and call the world back to the living God?

The next chapter will turn to the question of discernment: how Christians can learn to recognize the difference between the Spirit of God and the counterfeit "light" offered by the enemy, especially when that counterfeit cloaks itself in the language of love, justice, and progress.

Chapter 7

The Invisible War: Discerning Spirits and False Light

The Church does not suffer only from external enemies and internal scandals; she also suffers from confusion. Not every voice that speaks of love, justice, or inclusion is moved by the Spirit of God. Not every call for reform is truly prophetic. Not every appeal to mercy is faithful to truth. One of the devil's most effective strategies is to offer a counterfeit light, an imitation of goodness that mimics the language and tone of the Gospel while bending its content away from the cross. In an age saturated with competing moral visions, discerning the difference between the Holy Spirit and deceptive spirits is no luxury; it is a matter of spiritual survival.

Scripture warns repeatedly about this invisible war of voices. Believers are told to "test the spirits" because "many false prophets have gone out into the world." The danger is not primarily from open atheism or blatant occultism, but from teachings and movements that use Christian vocabulary while hollowing out its meaning. The apostle Paul warns that Satan disguises himself as an angel of light and that his servants can appear as servants of righteousness. This means that falsehood will rarely present itself as cruel, ugly, or obviously evil. Instead, it will present itself as more loving than God, more compassionate than Scripture, more reasonable than the apostles inviting the Church to "improve" the Gospel for the modern age.

True discernment begins with a fixed reference point. A sailor at sea cannot navigate by shifting waves; he must look to the stars. Likewise, Christians cannot navigate by feelings, fashions, or majority opinion; they must look to the unchanging Word of God. Any spirit, teaching, or movement that contradicts what God has revealed about Himself, His Son, and His commandments cannot come from Him, no matter how persuasive its advocates or how moving its rhetoric. The Holy Spirit never leads the Church to deny what He inspired in Scripture. He may deepen understanding, apply truth afresh, or correct misapplications, but He will not reverse God's clear moral law or contradict the apostolic witness.

At the same time, discernment is not merely an intellectual exercise. It is a moral and spiritual posture. A proud heart, enamored with its own insights, will easily mistake its preferences for the Spirit's leading. A fearful heart, desperate for cultural approval, will readily baptize the world's agenda as God's will. A bitter heart, wounded by hypocrisy, may embrace any movement that promises to overturn the old order, whether or not it aligns with Christ. For this reason, Scripture ties discernment to humility, obedience, and holiness. Those who wish to see clearly must be willing to submit their minds and desires to God, to repent when confronted by His Word, and to renounce sins that cloud judgment.

Several practical questions can help believers test the spirits. First: What does this teaching say about Jesus Christ? Does it confess Him as Lord, the unique Son of God, crucified and risen, the only Savior of sinners? Or does it reduce Him to a moral teacher, a symbol of inclusion, or one voice among many? Second: What does it say about sin and repentance? Does it call people to turn from specific sins and surrender their lives to God, or does it redefine sin as trauma, insist that God never asks anyone to change, and treat repentance as unhealthy guilt? Third: What does it say about Scripture? Does it treat the Bible as the authoritative Word of God, to which we must conform, or as a human document to be sifted, corrected, and selectively ignored?

Another test concerns the fruit produced over time. Jesus warns that false prophets can be known "by their fruits." This does not mean counting numbers or measuring popularity. It means asking: Does this teaching produce holiness, humility, courage, and love of God? Or does it produce confusion, moral compromise, spiritual pride, and contempt for those who remain faithful to traditional doctrine? Movements that bless what God forbids may initially appear compassionate, but their long-term fruit is often a weakened Church, disoriented believers, and a generation that no longer knows what repentance or sanctification mean.

Discernment also requires attention to pattern. A single misjudgment does not necessarily reveal a false spirit; even faithful leaders can err. But when a teacher, council, or denomination shows a consistent tendency to move in one direction, always toward relaxing moral demands, always toward aligning with secular opinion, never toward greater clarity or sacrifice, this pattern itself is a warning. The enemy rarely persuades the Church to leap into heresy in a single bound; he prefers gradual steps, each one presented as minor, pastoral, or provisional. The watchful disciple learns to recognize the trajectory, not just the isolated decision.

There is, however, a danger on the other side. In reacting against false light, some fall into paranoia. They begin to see deception everywhere, distrust all authority, and reject any development or nuance as compromise. This too serves the enemy, who is happy to fracture the Church through suspicion as surely as through error. True discernment does not mean rejecting all change or condemning all attempts to address new pastoral situations. It means holding fast to what is essential, those truths clearly taught in Scripture and received by the universal Church, while evaluating new proposals by that standard. Where Scripture is silent or leaves room for prudential judgment, believers must exercise charity and patience. Where Scripture speaks plainly, they must obey, regardless of cost.

In the present crises of Roman Catholicism and Anglicanism, this invisible war of spirits is evident. In Rome, some voices urge the Church to "evolve" on questions of sexuality, marriage, and the worthiness of communicants, often appealing to compassion while setting aside clear teachings. In Anglicanism, entire provinces have redefined sin as identity and blessing as a right, claiming the Spirit's guidance while departing from the Bible's moral vision. In both cases, the language of love has been used to justify what Scripture calls lawlessness. Discerning believers must resist the temptation to be swayed by sentiment alone; they must ask whether these developments reflect the mind of Christ or the whisper of another spirit.

What, then, does faithful discernment look like in practice? It involves several commitments. First, a life steeped in Scripture, reading, meditating, and allowing the Word to reshape instincts and desires. Second, participation in the sacramental and prayer life of the Church, where grace strengthens the soul against deception. Third, obedience in small things; those who habitually ignore God's commands in daily life will find it hard to recognize His voice in larger controversies. Fourth, seeking counsel from wise, holy, orthodox pastors and elders whose lives display the fruit of the Spirit. Lone rangers are easy prey; discernment is best exercised within the communion of the faithful.

Finally, discernment requires courage. Recognizing false light is one thing; standing against it is another. Those who refuse to bless what God forbids, or to affirm doctrines contrary to Scripture, will be accused of hardness, hatred, or backwardness. They may lose positions, friendships, or worldly respect. Yet this cost is not new. The prophets were always outnumbered by the court theologians; the apostles were frequently opposed by religious authorities. The invisible war of spirits is, in the end, a test of loyalty. Will the Church fear God or man? Will she trust the voice of her Shepherd or the applause of the crowd?

The chapters ahead will turn from diagnosis to remedy, from recognizing the enemy's strategies to embracing the path of repentance and renewal. Discernment is not an end in itself; it is the doorway to faithful action. Once the

Church sees that she is under assault not only from scandals and doctrinal novelties, but from subtle counterfeit lights, she must respond not with despair, but with a renewed clinging to the One who promised that His sheep will know His voice and not follow the stranger.

Chapter 8

Restoring the Fortress: Renewal Through Repentance

The exposure of sin within the Church, whether through scandal in Rome or doctrinal collapse in Canterbury, can tempt believers to despair. When priests betray their vows and bishops abandon the faith once delivered, it is easy to conclude that the fortress has already fallen, that the devil has finally breached the walls beyond repair. Yet Scripture offers a different interpretation. When God permits corruption to be exposed, He does so not to destroy His people, but to call them back. Judgment, the apostles remind us, begins with the household of God. The fire that burns away hypocrisy and compromise is painful, but it is also purifying. The true fortress of the Church is not her institutional strength, but her willingness to repent.

Repentance is not a public relations strategy; it is a spiritual act. It involves more than acknowledging "mistakes" or expressing regret over "mismanagement." Genuine repentance begins with calling sin by its proper name in the light of God's holiness. It is the prodigal son coming to himself and confessing, "I have sinned against heaven and before you," not merely, "I have made poor choices." For the Church, this means recognizing that covering up abuse, tolerating sexual immorality in the clergy, and rewriting God's moral law to suit the times are not unfortunate missteps; they are betrayals of Christ. Until this language is recovered, any talk of renewal will remain cosmetic.

True repentance also has a corporate dimension. While every individual will answer personally before God, the Church as an institution can and must confess the sins that have been committed in her name and under her authority. This does not mean that every member bears equal guilt, but it does mean that the Body suffers together. When a diocese hides abuse, when a province blesses what God forbids, when a synod votes to contradict Scripture, the whole communion is wounded. Corporate repentance, therefore, involves public acknowledgment of wrong, not only where crimes have been committed, but where doctrines and practices have strayed from the apostolic faith. Such confession may bring legal, financial, and reputational consequences, but the alternative is worse: continued alliance with the lies that opened the door to evil in the first place.

Repentance must be followed by concrete amendment of life. In the Roman context, this includes uncompromising policies that put the protection of children and vulnerable adults above the preservation of clerical status or institutional image. It means removing from ministry those who have violated trust, cooperating fully with civil authorities, and refusing to transfer known offenders to new assignments. It also requires reforming seminary formation to emphasize chastity, emotional maturity, and doctrinal fidelity, so that future priests are formed not as functionaries but as holy men of God. Where networks of secret sin or doctrinal dissent exist, they must be confronted and dismantled, not tolerated as necessary compromises.

For Anglicans, amendment of life entails returning to the

clear teaching of Scripture on sex, marriage, and holy orders. Provinces that have embraced revisionist doctrines must be called out, by faithful voices within and without, to renounce their errors and repent of the confusion they have sown. This call will not be welcomed; it may be ignored or resisted. Yet renewal cannot be built on a foundation of denial. Alternative structures and continuing jurisdictions must also examine themselves, guarding against the sins of pride, factionalism, and bitterness. It is not enough to be "not like them"; the measure of faithfulness is conformity to Christ, not distance from a fallen majority.

If repentance is the doorway, holiness is the architecture of the restored fortress. The Church does not defend herself primarily by stronger public relations or more sophisticated policies, but by the renewed pursuit of sanctity among clergy and laity alike. Holy priests, men who love God, embrace celibate chastity, preach the truth without compromise, and serve their flocks with humility, are one of heaven's chief answers to hell's infiltration. Holy bishops, shepherds who fear God more than governments or media, who discipline with justice and weep over the sins of their people are living rebukes to the spirit of the age. Holy laity, wives, husbands, single men and women, young and old embody in family, work, and parish life the very virtues the culture mocks.

Such holiness is not achieved by human effort alone. It is the work of grace, received through the ordinary means God has given, Word, sacrament, prayer, fasting, and fellowship. In times of crisis, there is a temptation to look for extraordinary interventions, a spectacular revival, a dramatic sign, a new movement promising quick restoration. God sometimes grants such moments, but more often He renews His Church through quiet fidelity: parishes where the liturgy is offered reverently, the Gospel is preached faithfully, confessions are heard, the poor are served, and Christians bear one another's burdens. The devil, who loves scandal and spectacle, finds such ordinary sanctity harder to exploit.

Another indispensable element of renewal is truthful speech. The Church cannot be restored while she continues to speak in evasions and euphemisms. Abuse must be called abuse, not "boundary crossing." Adultery and fornication must be named as sins, not merely "complex situations." Homosexual acts must be described in the language Scripture uses, rather than hidden behind vague calls for "accompaniment" that never mention repentance. Likewise, doctrinal error must be identified as such, even when it comes from respected theologians or high-ranking leaders. Truthful speech is costly; it can lead to conflict, loss of position, or ostracism. But the fortress cannot be rebuilt on half-truths.

At the same time, renewal cannot proceed on a foundation of hatred or contempt. Those who have fallen into grave sin or error are still human beings made in God's image, for whom Christ died. The call to repentance, whether addressed to an abusive priest, a complicit bishop, or a revisionist synod, must be framed not as a declaration of superiority, but as an urgent plea for salvation. Holiness that glories in the downfall of others is a counterfeit holiness; it plays into the enemy's desire to divide and devour. The Church must learn to hold together uncompromising moral clarity with genuine sorrow over sin, not only the sin "out there," but the sin "in here," in our own hearts and communities.

Ultimately, the restoration of the fortress is not a human project but a divine work. Christ remains the Lord of the Church, even when her visible structures are shaken. He walks among the lampstands, as Revelation portrays, commending what is good, rebuking what is evil, and calling His people to conquer by repentance and perseverance. The very fact that scandals have been dragged into the light, that doctrinal battles are being openly fought, is itself a sign that God is at work. The devil loves darkness and ambiguity; God exposes, divides, and refines. The question is not whether Christ will purify His Church, but whether those within her will submit to that purification or resist it.

In every age of crisis, God has raised up reformers, saints and movements that recall the Church to her first love. Some have worn habits, others cassocks, others plain clothes. Some have labored in high offices, others in obscure parishes. What unites them is a shared conviction that the answer to corruption is not abandonment of the Church, but deeper fidelity to her Lord. Today, Rome and Canterbury both stand in need of such reformers. They may be bishops, priests, deacons, or laypeople; they may labor within existing structures or alongside them. Their task will not be easy, but it will be necessary.

The devil has invested heavily in undermining the Church's

credibility and defiling her witness. He has had many successes. Yet he has overreached. The very excess of his attack has awakened many believers to the urgency of the hour. If the fortress is to be restored, it will not be by returning to business as usual, but by embracing the way of the cross, confession, cleansing, and costly obedience. The final chapter of this book will turn to the individual believer's role in this battle: how to build an unshakable faith amid shaking institutions, and how to stand firm in the armor of God while the war for the Church's soul continues.

Chapter 9

Building Unshakable Faith

When institutions tremble, believers face a stark choice. Either faith rests primarily on human structures, popes, bishops, synods, and councils, or it rests ultimately on Christ, who alone is the same yesterday, today, and forever. The scandals of Rome and the apostasy of large parts of Anglicanism have revealed how fragile earthly pillars can be. Yet they have also exposed a deeper truth: those whose faith is anchored in Christ and formed by His Word can stand firm even when trusted institutions falter. Unshakable faith is not blind to corruption; it is rooted in Someone greater than the corruption.

An unshakable faith begins with a clear understanding of what the Church is and is not. The Church is truly the Body of Christ, the household of God, and the pillar and ground of the truth. Yet her members, including her leaders, remain sinners in need of grace until the day of resurrection. No bishop's mitre, no priestly collar, no historic name on a church sign guarantees fidelity. When believers confuse Christ with His representatives or equate the purity of the Gospel with the outward stability of a particular institution, they are set up for disillusionment. Unshakable faith distinguishes between the infallible Lord and the fallible men who serve Him, refusing to excuse sin yet refusing also to abandon Christ because of Judas.

The apostle Paul's image of the armor of God offers a

practical blueprint for resilience. Truth girds the believer like a belt, holding everything else together. Righteousness, not merely imputed but increasingly lived, guards the heart like a breastplate. The Gospel of peace, internalized and cherished, equips the feet to move steadily through conflict. Faith itself acts as a shield, not by denying the reality of evil, but by trusting that God remains sovereign over it. Salvation, received and remembered, protects the mind from despair and cynicism. The Word of God, wielded as a sword, enables believers to counter the lies and half-truths that swirl around them. Prayer, constant and watchful, keeps the soldier in communication with the Commander.

In practice, building such faith requires intentional habits. Daily immersion in Scripture allows God's voice to become more familiar than the noise of media and controversy. Regular participation in the Church's worship, especially where Word and sacrament are treated with reverence roots the soul in a reality deeper than headlines. Confession of sin, both personal and corporate, keeps pride at bay and strengthens humility, which is a powerful defense against deception. Acts of charity, service, and self-sacrifice anchor faith in love, reminding believers that Christianity is not merely a set of ideas, but a life poured out for God and neighbor.

Community is essential. Isolated believers are more vulnerable to discouragement and error. In times of institutional upheaval, the temptation to withdraw entirely can be strong, especially for those burned by abuse or betrayed by leaders. Yet the answer to bad community is not no community, but better community. Small groups of believers who share a commitment to orthodoxy, holiness, and mutual support can become lifeboats in a storm-tossed sea. In such settings, doubts can be voiced without fear, wounds can be acknowledged, and burdens can be shared. The devil, who loves to pick off stragglers, finds it harder to isolate those who are surrounded by brothers and sisters.

Discernment, as described previously, must also be practiced personally. Each believer is called to test teachings they hear, even from respected voices, against the standard of Scripture and the consensus of the historic Church. If a sermon, policy, or directive contradicts the clear moral and doctrinal content of the faith, the disciple must obey God rather than men. This may mean quietly refusing to participate in certain practices, seeking out more faithful spiritual leadership, or in extreme cases separating from a compromised local body. Unshakable faith is not passive compliance; it is loyal first to Christ.

Suffering, paradoxically, often strengthens such faith. When holding to biblical truth brings loss of status, friendships, or opportunities, believers are forced to decide what matters most. Those who accept this cost learn, through experience, that God is faithful in affliction. Their faith moves from theory to endurance. Historically, times of persecution and crisis have produced some of the Church's greatest saints. While no one should seek suffering for its own sake, those who endure trial for righteousness' sake find that their trust in God becomes more robust, more realistic, and less dependent on favorable circumstances.

For Catholics and Anglicans who have watched their communions torn by scandal and compromise, building unshakable faith may require a painful reorientation. It might mean shifting from a primarily institutional loyalty to a Christ-centered loyalty, while still loving and praying for their church bodies. It might mean learning from faithful voices outside their accustomed circles. It might mean rethinking unspoken assumptions that "this church could never fall" or "our structures guarantee orthodoxy." Such illusions must die if faith is to mature. A fortress built on sentiment will not stand; one built on truth and repentance will.

Ultimately, the goal is not to produce hardened cynics who trust no one, but mature disciples who trust God above everyone. These disciples can honor faithful leaders without idolizing them, support institutions without ignoring their faults, and remain in the Church without being blind to her sins. They know that Christ has promised to be with His Church to the end of the age, but they also know that He sometimes removes lampstands that refuse to repent. Their hope, therefore, is not that "things will always go back to the way they were," but that God will continue to purify, prune, and preserve a people for Himself.

Unshakable faith looks beyond the present battle. The devil's aggression, visible in the scandals of Rome and the apostasies of Canterbury, is real and grievous. Yet it is also a sign of his desperation. A defeated enemy fights fiercest when his time is short. Believers who grasp this can view the Church's current trials not as proof of Christ's absence, but as arenas in which His victory will be manifested. They can pray, work, repent, and stand, knowing that no matter how many fortresses crumble, the kingdom cannot be shaken, and the captain of their salvation will not abandon His own.

Chapter 10

The Final Battle and the Faithful Remnant

History is moving toward a conclusion. The struggles of Rome and Canterbury, the corruption of clergy, the confusion of doctrine, and the culture's revolt against God are not isolated events; they are episodes in a larger war whose outcome has already been decided at the cross and will be fully revealed when Christ returns. The devil rages precisely because his time is short. His assaults on the Church through scandal, false teaching, and moral collapse are the desperate blows of a defeated foe. To see the present crisis rightly is to place it within that larger story: the story of a Bride being purified, an enemy being unmasked, and a kingdom drawing near.

The book of Revelation offers the clearest biblical window into this final conflict. There the dragon, identified as "that ancient serpent" and "the deceiver of the whole world," wages war against the saints, seeking to devour, deceive, and destroy. He uses beastly powers, political systems hostile to Christ and a false prophet; religious voices that legitimize idolatry to pressure believers into compromise. Yet again and again, the vision shows that the Lamb stands at the center. Those who follow Him may suffer, but they are sealed, preserved, and ultimately vindicated. The Church's path in history is not one of unbroken institutional triumph, but of faithful witness under fire, culminating in resurrection and glory.

In this light, the scandals and apostasies of our time reveal both the ferocity and the limits of the enemy's power. He can infiltrate chanceries and synods, twist the minds of theologians, seduce bishops and priests, and drag the Church's name through the mud. But he cannot overthrow Christ, revoke the promises of God, or prevent the Holy Spirit from preserving a faithful remnant. Even as some structures rot, others are renewed. Even as some leaders fall, others stand. The visible shape of the Church may change, new alignments form, old institutions crumble but the reality of the Church, as the company of those who hold to the testimony of Jesus and keep God's commandments, endures.

The faithful remnant, scattered across communions and continents, is not defined by perfect agreement on secondary matters, but by steadfast adherence to the essentials: the Lordship of Christ, the authority of Scripture, the call to holiness, and the centrality of the cross. In times of peace, it is easy for nominal Christianity to flourish; churches fill with those carried along by custom or culture. In times of shaking, that nominal layer is stripped away. Those who remain are those willing to endure misunderstanding, marginalization, and loss rather than deny the truth. This purification is painful, but it is also an act of mercy. Better a smaller, faithful Church than a vast body hollowed out by unbelief.

The final battle is not fought with swords or political power, but with fidelity. Ordinary believers, priests hearing confessions in forgotten parishes, parents teaching children the faith at the kitchen table, single men and women living chastely, monks and nuns praying unseen, laity who refuse to repeat lies even when everyone expects them to, are the Lord's chosen instruments. The world may never know their names. History books may record the headlines of scandal and schism but ignore the quiet heroism of those who simply refused to bow to the idols of the age. In heaven's ledger, however, these are the overcomers, the ones who "did not love their lives even unto death."

The Church's hope, therefore, is not that this or that institution will be restored to former prestige, but that Christ will complete the work He has begun in His people. Perhaps some great reversals will occur: Rome may yet experience a deep purification; Anglicanism may yet see a surprising renewal from the margins. Or perhaps not. Perhaps some structures will continue to decline while others, less noticed, become new vessels for God's work. What matters is not the survival of particular corporate forms, but the perseverance of faith, the proclamation of the true Gospel, and the sanctification of souls.

For individual believers, living in the shadow of the final battle means cultivating three virtues above all: vigilance, courage, and hope. Vigilance watches the times with clear eyes, recognizing where the enemy is at work and refusing both naïve optimism and paralyzing fear. Courage stands firm in truth, even when it brings cost, trusting that obedience is safer than compromise, no matter how risky it appears. Hope looks beyond the immediate battlefield to the promised end, when every tear will be wiped away, every injustice judged, and every faithful act, however hidden, brought to light.

The devil has indeed been active in this age, striking fiercely at the Roman Catholic and Anglican communions, exploiting their weaknesses, magnifying their sins, and seeking to turn their failures into arguments against the Gospel itself. But his malice cannot undo God's faithfulness. The same Lord who allowed Peter to fall and Judas to betray also restored Peter and judged Judas. The same Spirit who exposed the corruption of Eli's sons raised up Samuel. The same Christ who warned that wolves would arise in the flock also promised that His sheep would hear His voice and that no one could snatch them from His hand.

As this book closes, the call is simple and it is uncompromising. Do not deny or minimize the reality of the devil's work. Do not pretend that Rome's scandals or Canterbury's apostasies are minor misunderstandings, they cannot be so. However, do not surrender to despair. Instead, let the sight of these wounds drive you deeper into Christ and into His Word, His sacraments, His cross, and His coming kingdom. Stand where countless saints before you have stood: aware of the enemy, honest about the Church's sins, yet unshaken in the conviction that the Lamb who was slain is also the King who will reign, and that His Church, purified through fire, will one day be presented to Him without spot or wrinkle, shining with a beauty no scandal can erase and no devil can destroy.

Epilogue

The Serpent and the Bride

The Church walks through history with a limp. On one side is the scar of her own sin, abuse, betrayal, cowardice, compromise. On the other is the mark of her suffering at the hands of the world, persecution, ridicule, and contempt. From a purely human vantage point, it can be hard to see anything else. Newspapers record the scandals. Commentators tally the defections. Former believers recount their wounds. The serpent seems to have done his work well. And yet, beneath and beyond that visible story, another story is unfolding, the story of a Bride who, though wounded, is being purified for the day of her Lord.

This book has argued that the devil is not a distant myth, nor an outdated metaphor, but an intelligent adversary aggressively active against the Church in every generation. In ours, he has struck with particular force at the Roman Catholic and Anglican communions, exploiting their weaknesses, amplifying their sins, and turning their failures into stumbling blocks for many. His strategy has been consistent: infiltrate leadership, corrupt sexual morality, confuse doctrine, and harness the language of love and justice to justify rebellion against God. He has used the tools of relativism, sexual liberation, and self-idolatry to reshape minds, even within the sanctuary. He has done great damage.

Yet the serpent's power, however great it appears, is

always parasitic. He cannot create; he can only twist. He cannot finally destroy the Church; he can only wound her. His apparent victories are, in the light of eternity, temporary and self-defeating. Each scandal he engineers, each false teaching he advances, becomes in God's providence an occasion for exposure, repentance, and refinement. The same fire that reveals corruption also purifies what is true. When hidden sins are dragged into the light, when compromised doctrines provoke faithful resistance, when institutions shake and nominal believers fall away, what emerges slowly, painfully, is a smaller but truer Church, more aware of her dependence on grace.

The faithful remnant is not glamorous. It consists of believers who keep praying when others give up, who keep confessing when others rationalize, who keep obeying when others adjust the Gospel to fit the times. It includes priests who live their vows quietly and purely, far from headlines. It includes bishops who, against pressure, refuse to bless what God forbids. It includes lay men and women who teach their children the faith at home, even when their parish or denomination falters. It includes those who have been deeply hurt by the Church yet refuse to let the devil have the last word by driving them into unbelief. These are the ones who, in ways often unseen, frustrate the serpent's designs.

The final word over the Church does not belong to scandal or schism. It belongs to Christ. He is the One who walks among the lampstands, who searches hearts, who opens what no one can shut and shuts what no one can open. He is the Lamb who was slain and yet reigns, the Shepherd who lays down His life for the sheep and will lose none of those the Father has given Him. He is the bridegroom who will, at the end of all things, present to Himself a Bride "without spot or wrinkle," not because she has never sinned, but because He has washed her with His own blood.

Until that day, the Church lives in the tension of warfare and promise. The serpent is still in the sanctuary, whispering in ears, courting leaders, sowing divisions, and masquerading as an angel of light. The Bride is still being cleansed, often through humiliations she would never have chosen. The battlefield runs through chanceries and synods, yes, but also through every human heart. Each believer must decide, again and again, whom to trust, whom to fear, and whom to follow.

If there is one lesson to carry from these pages, it is this: do not be surprised by the devil's rage, and do not be shaken by the Church's wounds. The enemy is real and ruthless, but he is already judged. The Church is flawed and frequently faithless, but she is loved with an everlasting love. The call to every Christian, Catholic, Anglican, or otherwise is to stand in that paradox with open eyes and steadfast heart: grieving the sins that have given the serpent room to work, resisting the lies that would dress disobedience as compassion, and clinging more tightly than ever to the Cross where the decisive victory has already been won.

The serpent will not have the last word. The Bride will. And her final song will not be about her cleverness, her structures, or her leaders, but about the Lamb who rescued her from every snare, purified her through every trial, and brought her, at last, safely home.

Chapter 11

The ABC issue

As the final draft of this book was being edited a substantial change took place in the Church of England, which has the potential to create yet more schism in an already fractured communion.

The appointment of a woman as Archbishop of Canterbury both sharpens an already severe crisis for conservative Anglicans and opens new possibilities for reform, mission, and clarity about what "Anglican" now means globally. For the wider Communion, it accelerates an emerging realignment in which Canterbury becomes only one voice among many, rather than the uncontested symbolic center it once was.

We must look at this event in the light of all that has preceded in this book. A small change of direction for the Church of England, in light of their existing avoidance of all things scriptural. However, the impact of this change has already prompted strongly worded releases from many African Diocese and even National churches. If division was the goal again, it may have been achieved.

Setting the scene

The Church of England has only allowed women as bishops since 2014, but many Global South provinces still reject female episcopal headship on biblical and theological grounds.

The naming of Sarah Mullally as the first female Archbishop of Canterbury has become a lightning rod because it coincides with deep disputes over sexuality, biblical authority, and ecclesial identity.

Conservative Anglican concerns

For many conservative Anglicans, especially in Africa and parts of Asia, a female Archbishop of Canterbury is read as a public rejection of male-only oversight taught by Scripture and catholic tradition, not a marginal " adiaphoron." Leaders in GAFCON and the Global South Fellowship of Anglican Churches (GSFA) argue that this makes Canterbury incapable of functioning as a **focus** of communion, since a majority of Anglicans now cannot receive her ministry as consistent with apostolic order.

Statements from GAFCON and GSFA describe the appointment as "double jeopardy": it both ignores provinces that reject women bishops and elevates a leader identified with same-sex blessings and liberal bioethics.

Some conservative leaders formally reject the Archbishop of Canterbury's authority and urge their provinces to alter canons to remove any reference to communion with the See of Canterbury.

For these conservatives, the issue is not simply gender but what it symbolizes: a Church of England that, in their view, has surrendered biblical authority and historic Anglican teaching to Western cultural norms. The result is a strengthening of parallel conservative structures (GAFCON, GSFA, new "conservative Anglican" bodies) that claim to represent authentic Anglicanism apart from Canterbury.

Conservative arguments in favor

There is also a conservative argument that, paradoxically, the appointment may yield a "tragic clarity" that ultimately serves orthodox Anglicans. Some contend that Canterbury's choice confirms what has long been suspected: the official instruments of communion are no longer doctrinally reliable and therefore must be relativized.

By making the symbolic break so visible, the decision pushes conservatives to move from protest to constructive institution-building: new councils, confession-based covenants, and mission partnerships clearly rooted in Scripture and the classic Anglican formularies.

A few conservative voices note that their primary concern is the archbishop's theology, not her sex; they argue that a theologically orthodox woman in the role might have been tolerated, which forces conservatives to articulate more carefully what is essential and what is secondary.

From this angle, the appointment becomes a catalyst for repentance from "Canterbury-dependence" and an opportunity to re-centre authority on Scripture and conciliar agreement among confessing provinces rather than on an English See shaped by secular British politics.

75

Arguments welcoming the appointment

Those who welcome a female Archbishop of Canterbury—both moderates and progressives—see it as a natural development of Anglican commitments to human dignity, the baptismal equality of men and women, and the discernment of gifts without regard to sex. For them, retaining male-only leadership is itself a betrayal of biblical justice and the church's mission to a world that rightly rejects patriarchal exclusion.

Supporters argue that women have already been serving as priests and bishops for decades in many provinces; placing a woman at Canterbury simply aligns the symbolic center with the lived practice of large parts of the Communion.

Some female bishops, including in Africa, explicitly contest the idea that rejecting women's episcopacy is "biblical," calling such opposition a cultural patriarchy that harms the church's witness and ignores how God is using women in evangelism and pastoral care.

From this perspective, controversy is inevitable but not decisive: the Communion has always contained deep disagreements, and growth often occurs when justice-oriented reforms are embraced despite initial schism.

Outcomes for the global Anglican Church

In the near term, the appointment intensifies visible schism: GAFCON and allied provinces distance themselves further, some formally claiming that "we are the Anglican Communion" while rejecting Canterbury's moral and doctrinal leadership. The Archbishop of Canterbury becomes a "first among unequals," accepted by some provinces, tolerated by others, and refused by a growing conservative bloc.

The likely structural outcome is a looser, multi-polar Anglican world: Canterbury-aligned churches; a robust conservative network centered on GAFCON/GSFA; and smaller overlapping jurisdictions in the West and Global South.

Ecumenically, the move complicates relations with Rome and some Orthodox churches that see women's ordination as a serious obstacle, even as it may encourage internal Catholic debates over women's roles.

In the longer term, two paths become visible. One is a de facto permanent split in which "Anglican" names a family of related but non-intercommunicating churches sorted by their responses to Scripture, sexuality, and women's orders. The other is a painful but clarifying season that eventually yields new conciliar structures, where communion is grounded less in historical ties to Canterbury and more in shared confession and mission, with the female Archbishop of Canterbury recognized as one significant, but not determinative, leader in a fractured yet still recognizably Anglican world.

At a time like this I can see our most powerful choice is for prayer and the final page contains a prayer written by the author, as Primate of the Conservative Anglican Communion. May God bless you.

Merciful and Almighty God,
Lord of the Church and Head of the Body,

In this hour of confusion and grief, turn Your face toward Your servants who long to be faithful to Your Word.
Grant to conservative Anglicans around the world grace to stand firm upon the Scriptures, to love the truth without bitterness, and to guard their hearts from despair or hatred.

Lord Jesus, Good Shepherd,
You purchased the Church with Your own blood.
When shepherds fail and leaders depart from the pattern of sound teaching, keep Your flock from stumbling.
Strengthen bishops, priests, deacons, and laity who seek to remain obedient to the plain teaching of Your Word and the good order of the apostolic Church.
Give them courage to confess the faith once delivered to the saints, with humility, clarity, and charity.

Holy Spirit, Spirit of truth,
Expose what is contrary to the Scriptures, and purify Your Church.
Protect Your people from false teaching and from the temptation to compromise in order to avoid suffering.
Yet also save them from pride, from schismatic anger, and from delighting in the fall of others.
Let repentance begin with all of us, and renew in us a deep hunger for holiness, prayer, and sacrificial love.

Heavenly Father,
Raise up godly pastors and teachers who will feed Your flock with sound doctrine, reverent worship, and lives marked by integrity.
Prosper every effort to build and sustain biblically faithful Anglican communities, at home and across the nations.
May their witness be marked not only by orthodoxy of belief but by conspicuous compassion for the poor, the broken, and the lost.

Grant that, in the midst of institutional shaking, Your people may find their security not in earthly offices or titles, but in Christ alone—our great High Priest, our only Mediator, and our unfailing Rock.
Keep us steadfast in truth, joyful in hope, fervent in prayer, and patient in suffering, until that day when every error is corrected, every tear is wiped away, and the whole Church, purified and united, shall worship You in everlasting light.

Through Jesus Christ our Lord,
who lives and reigns with You and the Holy Spirit,
one God, world without end.
Amen.

www.ingramcontent.com/pod-product-compliance
Lightning Source LLC
LaVergne TN
LVHW020937090426
835512LV00020B/3406